Collected Poems, 1897-1907

Henry Newbolt

To Thomas Hardy

Drake's Drum

Drake he's in his hammock an' a thousand miles away,
  (Capten, art tha sleepin' there below?)
Slung atween the round shot in Nombre Dios Bay,
  An' dreamin' arl the time O' Plymouth Hoe.
Yarnder lumes the Island, yarnder lie the ships,
  Wi' sailor lads a-dancing' heel-an'-toe,
An' the shore-lights flashin', an' the night-tide dashin',
  He sees et arl so plainly as he saw et long ago.

Drake he was a Devon man, an' rüled the Devon seas,
  (Capten, art tha' sleepin' there below?)
Roving' tho' his death fell, he went wi' heart at ease,
  An' dreamin' arl the time o' Plymouth Hoe.
"Take my drum to England, hang et by the shore,
  Strike et when your powder's runnin' low;
If the Dons sight Devon, I'll quit the port o' Heaven,
  An' drum them up the Channel as we drummed them long ago."

Drake he's in his hammock till the great Armadas come,
  (Capten, art tha sleepin' there below?)
Slung atween the round shot, listenin' for the drum,
  An' dreamin arl the time o' Plymouth Hoe.
Call him on the deep sea, call him up the Sound,
  Call him when ye sail to meet the foe;
Where the old trade's plyin' an' the old flag flyin'
  They shall find him ware an' wakin', as they found him long ago!

The Fighting Téméraire

It was eight bells ringing,
  For the morning watch was done,
And the gunner's lads were singing
  As they polished every gun.
It was eight bells ringing,
And the gunner's lads were singing,
For the ship she rode a-swinging,
  As they polished every gun.

  Oh! to see the linstock lighting,
    Téméraire! Téméraire!
  Oh! to hear the round shot biting,
    Téméraire! Téméraire!

  Oh! to see the linstock lighting,
    And to hear the round shot biting,
  For we're all in love with fighting
    On the fighting Téméraire.

It was noontide ringing,
  And the battle just begun,
When the ship her way was winging,
  As they loaded every gun.
It was noontide ringing,
When the ship her way was winging,
And the gunner's lads were singing
  As they loaded every gun.

  There'll be many grim and gory,
    Téméraire! Téméraire!
  There'll be few to tell the story,
    Téméraire! Téméraire!

  There'll be many grim and gory,
    There'll be few to tell the story,
  But we'll all be one in glory
    With the Fighting Téméraire.

There's a far bell ringing
  At the setting of the sun,
And a phantom voice is singing
  Of the great days done.
There's a far bell ringing,
And a phantom voice is singing
Of renown for ever clinging
  To the great days done.

    Now the sunset breezes shiver,
      Téméraire! Téméraire!
    And she's fading down the river,
      Téméraire! Téméraire!

    Now the sunset's breezes shiver,
      And she's fading down the river,
    But in England's song for ever
      She's the Fighting Téméraire.

Admirals All

Effingham, Grenville, Raleigh, Drake,
  Here's to the bold and free!
Benbow, Collingwood, Byron, Blake,
  Hail to the Kings of the Sea!
Admirals all, for England's sake,
  Honour be yours and fame!
And honour, as long as waves shall break,
  To Nelson's peerless name!

  Admirals all, for England's sake,
    Honour be yours and fame!
  And honour, as long as waves shall break,
    To Nelson's peerless name!

Essex was fretting in Cadiz Bay
  With the galleons fair in sight;
Howard at last must give him his way,
  And the word was passed to fight.
Never was schoolboy gayer than he,
  Since holidays first began:
He tossed his bonnet to wind and sea,
  And under the guns he ran.

Drake nor devil nor Spaniard feared,
  Their cities he put to the sack;
He singed his Catholic Majesty's beard,
  And harried his ships to wrack.
He was playing at Plymouth a rubber of bowls
  When the great Armada came;
But he said, "They must wait their turn, good souls,"
  And he stooped and finished the game.

Fifteen sail were the Dutchmen bold,
  Duncan he had but two;
But he anchored them fast where the Texel shoaled,
  And his colours aloft he flew.
"I've taken the depth to a fathom," he cried,
  "And I'll sink with a right good will:
For I know when we're all of us under the tide
  My flag will be fluttering still."

Splinters were flying above, below,
  When Nelson sailed the Sound:
"Mark you, I wouldn't be elsewhere now,"
  Said he, "for a thousand pound!"
The Admiral's signal bade him fly
  But he wickedly wagged his head:
He clapped the glass to his sightless eye,
  And "I'm damned if I see it!" he said.

Admirals all, they said their say
  (The echoes are ringing still).
Admirals all, they went their way
  To the haven under the hill.
But they left us a kingdom none can take,
  The realm of the circling sea,
To be ruled by the rightful sons of Blake,
  And the Rodneys yet to be.

    Admirals all, for England's sake,
      Honour be yours and fame!
    And honour, as long as waves shall break,
      To Nelson's peerless name!

San Stefano

(A Ballad of the Bold Menelaus)

It was morning at St. Helen's, in the great and gallant days,
  And the sea beneath the sun glittered wide,
When the frigate set her courses, all a-shimmer in the haze
  And she hauled her cable home and took the tide.
She'd a right fighting company, three hundred men and more,
  Nine and forty guns in tackle running free;
And they cheered her from the shore for her colours at the fore,
  When the bold *Menelaus* put to sea.

  She'd a right fighting company, three hundred men and more,
    Nine and forty guns in tackle running free;
  And they cheered her from the shore for her colours at the fore,
    When the bold *Menelaus* put to sea.

She was clear of Monte Cristo, she was heading for the land,
  When she spied a pennant red and white and blue;
They were foemen, and they knew it, and they'd half a league in hand,
  But she flung aloft her royals, and she flew.
She was nearer, nearer, nearer, they were caught beyond a doubt,
  But they slipped her into Orbetello Bay,
And the lubbers gave a shout as they paid their cables out,
  With the guns grinning round them where they lay.

Now, Sir Peter was a captain of a famous fighting race,
  Son and grandson of an admiral was he;
And he looked upon the batteries, he looked upon the chase,
  And he heard the shout that echoed out to sea.
And he called across the decks, "Ay! the cheering might be late
  If they kept it till the *Menelaus* runs;
Bid the master and his mate heave the lead and lay her straight
  For the prize lying yonder by the guns!"

When the summer moon was setting, into Orbetello Bay
  Came the *Menelaus* gliding like a ghost;
And her boats were manned in silence, and in silence pulled away,
  And in silence every gunner took his post.
With a volley from her broadside the citadel she woke,
  And they hammered back like heroes all the night;

But before the morning broke she had vanished through the smoke
  With her prize upon her quarter grappled tight.

It was evening at St. Helen's in the great and gallant time,
  And the sky behind the down was flushing far;
And the flags were all a-flutter, and the bells were all a-chime,
  When the frigate cast her anchor off the bar.
She'd a right fighting company, three hundred men and more,
  Nine and forty guns in tackle running free;
And they cheered her from the shore for the colours at the fore,
  When the bold *Menelaus* came from the sea.

  She'd a right fighting company, three hundred men and more,
    Nine and forty guns in tackle running free;
  And they cheered her from the shore for her colours at the fore,
    When the bold *Menelaus* came from the sea.

Hawke

In seventeen hundred and fifty-nine,
  When Hawke came swooping from the West,
The French King's Admiral with twenty of the line,
  Was sailing forth to sack us, out of Brest.
The ports of France were crowded, the quays of France a-hum
With thirty thousand soldiers marching to the drum,
For bragging time was over and fighting time was come
  When Hawke came swooping from the West.

'Twas long past noon of a wild November day
  When Hawke came swooping from the West;
He heard the breakers thundering in Quiberon Bay,
  But he flew the flag for battle, line abreast.
Down upon the quicksands roaring out of sight
Fiercely beat the storm-wind, darkly fell the night,
But they took the foe for pilot and the cannon's glare for light
  When Hawke came swooping from the West.

The Frenchmen turned like a covey down the wind
  When Hawke came swooping from the West;
One he sank with all hands, one he caught and pinned,
  And the shallows and the storm took the rest.
The guns that should have conquered us they rusted on the shore,
The men that would have mastered us they drummed and marched no more,
For England was England, and a mighty brood she bore
  When Hawke came swooping from the West.

The Bright Medusa

(1807)

She's the daughter of the breeze,
She's the darling of the seas,
  And we call her, if you please, the bright *Medu*—*sa*;
From beneath her bosom bare
To the snakes among her hair
  She's a flash o' golden light, the bright *Medu*—*sa*.

When the ensign dips above
And the guns are all for love,
  She's as gentle as a dove, the bright *Medu*—*sa*;
But when the shot's in rack
And her forestay flies the Jack,
  He's a merry man would slight the bright *Medu*—*sa*.

When she got the word to go
Up to Monte Video,
  There she found the river low, the bright *Medu*—*sa*;
So she tumbled out her guns
And a hundred of her sons,
  And she taught the Dons to fight the bright *Medu*—*sa*.

When the foeman can be found
With the pluck to cross her ground,
  First she walks him round and round, the bright *Medu*—*sa*;
Then she rakes him fore and aft
Till he's just a jolly raft,
  And she grabs him like a kite, the bright *Medu*—*sa*.

She's the daughter of the breeze,
She's the darling of the seas,
  And you'll call her, if you please, the bright *Medu*—*sa*;
For till England's sun be set—
And it's not for setting yet—
  She shall bear her name by right, the bright *Medu*—*sa*.

The Old Superb

The wind was rising easterly, the morning sky was blue,
  The Straits before us opened wide and free;
We looked towards the Admiral, where high the Peter flew,
  And all our hearts were dancing like the sea.
"The French are gone to Martinique with four and twenty sail!
  The Old *Superb* is old and foul and slow,
But the French are gone to Martinique, and Nelson's on the trail.
  And where he goes the Old *Superb* must go!"

    So Westward ho! for Trinidad, and Eastward ho! for Spain,
      And "Ship ahoy!" a hundred times a day;
     Round the world if need be, and round the world again,
      With a lame duck lagging all the way.

The Old *Superb* was barnacled and green as grass below,
  Her sticks were only fit for stirring grog;
The pride of all her midshipmen was silent long ago,
  And long ago they ceased to heave the log.
Four year out from home she was, and ne'er a week in port,
  And nothing save the guns aboard her bright;
But Captain Keats he knew the game, and swore to share the sport,
  For he never yet came in too late to fight.

    So Westward ho! for Trinidad, and Eastward ho! for Spain,
      And "Ship ahoy!" a hundred times a day;
     Round the world if need be, and round the world again,
      With a lame duck lagging all the way.

"Now up, my lads," the Captain cried, "for sure the case were hard
  If longest out were first to fall behind;
Aloft, aloft with studding sails, and lash them on the yard,
  For night and day the Trades are driving blind!"
So all day long and all day long behind the fleet we crept,
  And how we fretted none but Nelson guessed;
But every night the Old *Superb* she sailed when others slept,
  Till we ran the French to earth with all the rest.

    Oh, 'twas Westward ho! for Trinidad, and Eastward ho! for Spain,
      And "Ship ahoy!" a hundred times a day;
     Round the world if need be, and round the world again,
      With a lame duck lagging all the way.

The Quarter-Gunner's Yarn

We lay at St. Helen's, and easy she rode
With one anchor catted and fresh-water stowed;
When the barge came alongside like bullocks we roared,
For we knew what we carried with Nelson aboard.

Our Captain was Hardy, the pride of us all,
I'll ask for none better when danger shall call;
He was hardy by nature and Hardy by name,
And soon by his conduct to honour he came.

The third day the Lizard was under our lee,
Where the *Ajax* and *Thunderer* joined us at sea,
But what with foul weather and tacking about,
When we sighted the Fleet we were thirteen days out.

The Captains they all came aboard quick enough,
But the news that they brought was as heavy as duff;
So backward an enemy never was seen,
They were harder to come at than Cheeks the Marine.

The lubbers had hare's lugs where seamen have ears,
So we stowed all saluting and smothered our cheers,
And to humour their stomachs and tempt them to dine,
In the offing we showed them but six of the line.

One morning the topmen reported below
The old *Agamemnon* escaped from the foe.
Says Nelson: "My lads, there'll be honour for some,
For we're sure of a battle now Berry has come."

"Up hammocks!" at last cried the bo'sun at dawn;
The guns were cast loose and the tompions drawn;
The gunner was bustling the shot racks to fill,
And "All hands to quarters!" was piped with a will.

We now saw the enemy bearing ahead,
And to East of them Cape Traflagar it was said,
'Tis a name we remember from father to son,
That the days of old England may never be done.

The *Victory* led, to her flag it was due,
Tho' the *Téméraires* thought themselves Admirals too;
But Lord Nelson he hailed them with masterful grace:
"Cap'n Harvey, I'll thank you to keep in your place."

To begin with we closed the *Bucentaure* alone,
An eighty-gun ship and their Admiral's own;
We raked her but once, and the rest of the day
Like a hospital hulk on the water she lay.

To our battering next the *Redoutable* struck,
But her sharpshooters gave us the worst of the luck:
Lord Nelson was wounded, most cruel to tell.
"They've done for me; Hardy!" he cried as he fell.

To the cockpit in silence they carried him past,
And sad were the looks that were after him cast;
His face with a kerchief he tried to conceal,
But we knew him too well from the truck to the keel.

When the Captain reported a victory won,
"Thank God!" he kept saying, "my duty I've done."
At last came the moment to kiss him good-bye,
And the Captain for once had the salt in his eye.

"Now anchor, dear Hardy," the Admiral cried;
But before we could make it he fainted and died.
All night in the trough of the sea we were tossed,
And for want of ground-tackle good prizes were lost.

Then we hauled down the flag, at the fore it was red,
And blue at the mizzen was hoisted instead
By Nelson's famed Captain, the pride of each tar,
Who fought in the *Victory* off Cape Traflagar.

Northumberland

"The Old and Bold"

When England sets her banner forth
  And bids her armour shine,
She'll not forget the famous North,
  The lads of moor and Tyne;
And when the loving-cup's in hand,
  And Honour leads the cry,
They know not old Northumberland
  Who'll pass her memory by.

When Nelson sailed for Trafalgar
  With all his country's best,
He held them dear as brothers are,
  But one beyond the rest.
For when the fleet with heroes manned
  To clear the decks began,
The boast of old Northumberland
  He sent to lead the van.

Himself by *Victory's* bulwarks stood
  And cheered to see the sight;
"That noble fellow Collingwood,
  How bold he goes to fight!"
Love, that the league of Ocean spanned,
  Heard him as face to face;
"What would he give, Northumberland,
  To share our pride of place?"

The flag that goes the world around
  And flaps on every breeze
Has never gladdened fairer ground
  Or kinder hearts than these.
So when the loving-cup's in hand
  And Honour leads the cry,
They know not old Northumberland
  Who'll pass her memory by.

For A Trafalgar Cenotaph

Lover of England, stand awhile and gaze
With thankful heart, and lips refrained from praise;
They rest beyond the speech of human pride
Who served with Nelson and with Nelson died.

Craven

(Mobile Bay, 1864)

Over the turret, shut in his iron-clad tower,
　Craven was conning his ship through smoke and flame;
Gun to gun he had battered the fort for an hour,
　Now was the time for a charge to end the game.

There lay the narrowing channel, smooth and grim,
　A hundred deaths beneath it, and never a sign;
There lay the enemy's ships, and sink or swim
　The flag was flying, and he was head of the line.

The fleet behind was jamming; the monitor hung
　Beating the stream; the roar for a moment hushed,
Craven spoke to the pilot; slow she swung;
　Again he spoke, and right for the foe she rushed.

Into the narrowing channel, between the shore
　And the sunk torpedoes lying in treacherous rank;
She turned but a yard too short; a muffled roar,
　A mountainous wave, and she rolled, righted, and sank.

Over the manhole, up in the iron-clad tower,
　Pilot and Captain met as they turned to fly:
The hundredth part of a moment seemed an hour,
　For one could pass to be saved, and one must die.

They stood like men in a dream: Craven spoke,
　Spoke as he lived and fought, with a Captain's pride,
"After you, Pilot." The pilot woke,
　Down the ladder he went, and Craven died.

　All men praise the deed and the manner, but we—-
　　We set it apart from the pride that stoops to the proud,
　The strength that is supple to serve the strong and free,
　　The grace of the empty hands and promises loud:

　Sidney thirsting, a humbler need to slake,
　　Nelson waiting his turn for the surgeon's hand,
　Lucas crushed with chains for a comrade's sake,
　　Outram coveting right before command:

These were paladins, these were Craven's peers,
  These with him shall be crowned in story and song,
Crowned with the glitter of steel and the glimmer of tears,
  Princes of courtesy, merciful, proud, and strong.

Messmates

He gave us all a good-bye cheerily
  At the first dawn of day;
We dropped him down the side full drearily
  When the light died away.
It's a dead dark watch that he's a-keeping there,
And a long, long night that lags a-creeping there,
Where the Trades and the tides roll over him
  And the great ships go by.

He's there alone with green seas rocking him
  For a thousand miles round;
He's there alone with dumb things mocking him,
  And we're homeward bound.
It's a long, lone watch that he's a-keeping there,
And a dead cold night that lags a-creeping there,
While the months and the years roll over him
  And the great ships go by.

I wonder if the tramps come near enough
  As they thrash to and fro,
And the battle-ships' bells ring clear enough
  To be heard down below;
If through all the lone watch that he's a-keeping there,
And the long, cold night that lags a-creeping there,
The voices of the sailor-men shall comfort him
  When the great ships go by.

The Death Of Admiral Blake

(August 7th, 1657)

Laden with spoil of the South, fulfilled with the glory of achievement,
  And freshly crowned with never-dying fame,
Sweeping by shores where the names are the names of the victories of England,
  Across the Bay the squadron homeward came.

Proudly they came, but their pride was the pomp of a funeral at midnight,
  When dreader yet the lonely morrow looms;
Few are the words that are spoken, and faces are gaunt beneath the torchlight
  That does but darken more the nodding plumes.

Low on the field of his fame, past hope lay the Admiral triumphant,
  And fain to rest him after all his pain;
Yet for the love that he bore to his own land, ever unforgotten,
  He prayed to see the western hills again.

Fainter than stars in a sky long gray with the coming of the daybreak,
  Or sounds of night that fade when night is done,
So in the death-dawn faded the splendour and loud renown of warfare,
  And life of all its longings kept but one.

"Oh! to be there for an hour when the shade draws in beside the hedgerows,
  And falling apples wake the drowsy noon:
Oh! for the hour when the elms grow sombre and human in the twilight,
  And gardens dream beneath the rising moon.

"Only to look once more on the land of the memories of childhood,
  Forgetting weary winds and barren foam:
Only to bid farewell to the combe and the orchard and the moorland,
  And sleep at last among the fields of home!"

So he was silently praying, till now, when his strength was ebbing faster,
  The Lizard lay before them faintly blue;
Now on the gleaming horizon the white cliffs laughed along the coast-line,
  And now the forelands took the shapes they knew.

There lay the Sound and the Island with green leaves down beside the water,
  The town, the Hoe, the masts with sunset fired — —
Dreams! ay, dreams of the dead! for the great heart faltered on the threshold,
  And darkness took the land his soul desired.

Væ Victis

Beside the placid sea that mirrored her
  With the old glory of dawn that cannot die,
The sleeping city began to moan and stir,
  As one that fain from an ill dream would fly;
  Yet more she feared the daylight bringing nigh
Such dreams as know not sunrise, soon or late,—-
  Visions of honour lost and power gone by,
  Of loyal valour betrayed by factious hate,
And craven sloth that shrank from the labour of forging fate.

They knew and knew not, this bewildered crowd,
  That up her streets in silence hurrying passed,
What manner of death should make their anguish loud,
  What corpse across the funeral pyre be cast,
  For none had spoken it; only, gathering fast
As darkness gathers at noon in the sun's eclipse,
  A shadow of doom enfolded them, vague and vast,
  And a cry was heard, unfathered of earthly lips,
"What of the ships, O Carthage? Carthage, what of the ships?"

They reached the wall, and nowise strange it seemed
  To find the gates unguarded and open wide;
They climbed the shoulder, and meet enough they deemed
  The black that shrouded the seaward rampart's side
  And veiled in drooping gloom the turrets' pride;
But this was nought, for suddenly down the slope
  They saw the harbour, and sense within them died;
  Keel nor mast was there, rudder nor rope;
It lay like a sea-hawk's eyry spoiled of life and hope.

Beyond, where dawn was a glittering carpet, rolled
  From sky to shore on level and endless seas,
Hardly their eyes discerned in a dazzle of gold
  That here in fifties, yonder in twos and threes,
  The ships they sought, like a swarm of drowning bees
By a wanton gust on the pool of a mill-dam hurled,
  Floated forsaken of life-giving tide and breeze,
  Their oars broken, their sails for ever furled,
For ever deserted the bulwarks that guarded the wealth of the world.

A moment yet, with breathing quickly drawn
  And hands agrip, the Carthaginian folk
Stared in the bright untroubled face of dawn,
  And strove with vehement heaped denial to choke
  Their sure surmise of fate's impending stroke;
Vainly—for even now beneath their gaze
  A thousand delicate spires of distant smoke
  Reddened the disc of the sun with a stealthy haze,
And the smouldering grief of a nation burst with the kindling blaze.

"O dying Carthage!" so their passion raved,
  "Would nought but these the conqueror's hate assuage?
If these be taken, how may the land be saved
  Whose meat and drink was empire, age by age?"
  And bitter memory cursed with idle rage
The greed that coveted gold beyond renown,
  The feeble hearts that feared their heritage,
  The hands that cast the sea-kings' sceptre down
And left to alien brows their famed ancestral crown.

The endless noon, the endless evening through,
  All other needs forgetting, great or small,
They drank despair with thirst whose torment grew
  As the hours died beneath that stifling pall.
  At last they saw the fires to blackness fall
One after one, and slowly turned them home,
  A little longer yet their own to call
  A city enslaved, and wear the bonds of Rome,
With weary hearts foreboding all the woe to come.

Minora Sidera

(The Dictionary Of National Biography)

Sitting at times over a hearth that burns
  With dull domestic glow,
My thought, leaving the book, gratefully turns
  To you who planned it so.

Not of the great only you deigned to tell —-
  The stars by which we steer —-
But lights out of the night that flashed, and fell
  Tonight again, are here.

Such as were those, dogs of an elder day,
  Who sacked the golden ports,
And those later who dared grapple their prey
  Beneath the harbour forts:

Some with flag at the fore, sweeping the world
  To find an equal fight,
And some who joined war to their trade, and hurled
  Ships of the line in flight.

Whether their fame centuries long should ring
  They cared not over-much,
But cared greatly to serve God and the king,
  And keep the Nelson touch;

And fought to build Britain above the tide
  Of wars and windy fate;
And passed content, leaving to us the pride
  Of lives obscurely great.

Laudabunt Alii

(After Horace)

Let others praise, as fancy wills,
  Berlin beneath her trees,
Or Rome upon her seven hills,
  Or Venice by her seas;
Stamboul by double tides embraced,
Or green Damascus in the waste.

For me there's nought I would not leave
  For the good Devon land,
Whose orchards down the echoing cleeve
  Bedewed with spray-drift stand,
And hardly bear the red fruit up
That shall be next year's cider-cup.

You too, my friend, may wisely mark
  How clear skies follow rain,
And, lingering in your own green park
  Or drilled on Laffan's Plain,
Forget not with the festal bowl
To soothe at times your weary soul.

When Drake must bid to Plymouth Hoe
  Good-bye for many a day,
And some were sad and feared to go,
  And some that dared not stay,
Be sure he bade them broach the best,
And raised his tankard with the rest.

"Drake's luck to all that sail with Drake
  For promised lands of gold!
Brave lads, whatever storms may break,
  We've weathered worse of old!
To-night the loving-cup we'll drain,
To-morrow for the Spanish Main!"

Admiral Death

Boys, are ye calling a toast to-night?
  (Hear what the sea-wind saith)
Fill for a bumper strong and bright,
  And here's to Admiral Death!
He's sailed in a hundred builds o' boat,
He's fought in a thousand kinds o' coat,
He's the senior flag of all that float,
  And his name's Admiral Death!

Which of you looks for a service free?
  (Hear what the sea-wind saith)
The rules o' the service are but three
  When ye sail with Admiral Death.
Steady your hand in time o' squalls,
Stand to the last by him that falls,
And answer clear to the voice that calls,
  "Ay, Ay! Admiral Death!"

How will ye know him among the rest?
  (Hear what the sea-wind saith)
By the glint o' the stars that cover his breast
  Ye may find Admiral Death.
By the forehead grim with an ancient scar,
By the voice that rolls like thunder far,
By the tenderest eyes of all that are,
  Ye may know Admiral Death.

Where are the lads that sailed before?
  (Hear what the sea-wind saith)
Their bones are white by many a shore,
  They sleep with Admiral Death.
Oh! but they loved him, young and old,
For he left the laggard, and took the bold,
And the fight was fought, and the story's told,
  And they sleep with Admiral Death.

Homeward Bound

After long labouring in the windy ways,
  On smooth and shining tides
  Swiftly the great ship glides,
    Her storms forgot, her weary watches past;
Northward she glides, and through the enchanted haze
    Faint on the verge her far hope dawns at last.

The phantom sky-line of a shadowy down,
  Whose pale white cliffs below
  Through sunny mist aglow,
    Like noon-day ghosts of summer moonshine gleam —-
Soft as old sorrow, bright as old renown,
    There lies the home, of all our mortal dream.

Gillespie.

Riding at dawn, riding alone,
  Gillespie left the town behind;
Before he turned by the Westward road
  A horseman crossed him, staggering blind.

"The Devil's abroad in false Vellore,
  The Devil that stabs by night," he said,
"Women and children, rank and file,
  Dying and dead, dying and dead."

Without a word, without a groan,
  Sudden and swift Gillespie turned,
The blood roared in his ears like fire,
  Like fire the road beneath him burned.

He thundered back to Arcot gate,
  He thundered up through Arcot town,
Before he thought a second thought
  In the barrack yard he lighted down.

"Trumpeter, sound for the Light Dragoons,
  Sound to saddle and spur," he said;
"He that is ready may ride with me,
  And he that can may ride ahead."

Fierce and fain, fierce and fain,
  Behind him went the troopers grim,
They rode as ride the Light Dragoons
  But never a man could ride with him.

Their rowels ripped their horses' sides,
  Their hearts were red with a deeper goad,
But ever alone before them all
  Gillespie rode, Gillespie rode.

Alone he came to false Vellore,
  The walls were lined, the gates were barred;
Alone he walked where the bullets bit,
  And called above to the Sergeant's Guard.

"Sergeant, Sergeant, over the gate,
  Where are your officers all?" he said;
Heavily came the Sergeant's voice,
  "There are two living and forty dead."

"A rope, a rope," Gillespie cried :
  They bound their belts to serve his need.
There was not a rebel behind the wall
  But laid his barrel and drew his bead.

There was not a rebel among them all
  But pulled his trigger and cursed his aim,
For lightly swung and rightly swung
  Over the gate Gillespie came.

He dressed the line, he led the charge,
  They swept the wall like a stream in spate,
And roaring over the roar they heard
  The galloper guns that burst the gate.

Fierce and fain, fierce and fain,
  The troopers rode the reeking flight:
The very stones remember still
  The end of them that stab by night.

They've kept the tale a hundred years,
  They'll keep the tale a hundred more:
Riding at dawn, riding alone,
  Gillespie came to false Vellore.

Seringapatam

"The sleep that Tippoo Sahib sleeps
  Heeds not the cry of man;
The faith that Tippoo Sahib keeps
  No judge on earth may scan;
He is the lord of whom ye hold
  Spirit and sense and limb,
Fetter and chain are all ye gain
  Who dared to plead with him."

Baird was bonny and Baird was young,
  His heart was strong as steel,
But life and death in the balance hung,
  For his wounds were ill to heal.
"Of fifty chains the Sultan gave
  We have filled but forty-nine:
We dare not fail of the perfect tale
  For all Golconda's mine."

That was the hour when Lucas first
  Leapt to his long renown;
Like summer rains his anger burst,
  And swept their scruples down.
"Tell ye the lord to whom ye crouch,
  His fetters bite their fill:
To save your oath I'll wear them both,
  And step the lighter still."

The seasons came, the seasons passed,
  They watched their fellows die;
But still their thought was forward cast,
  Their courage still was high.
Through tortured days and fevered nights
  Their limbs alone were weak,
And year by year they kept their cheer,
  And spoke as freemen speak.

But once a year, on the fourth of June,
  Their speech to silence died,
And the silence beat to a soundless tune
  And sang with a wordless pride;

Till when the Indian stars were bright,
  And bells at home would ring,
To the fetters' clank they rose and drank
  "England! God save the King!"

The years came, and the years went,
  The wheel full-circle rolled;
The tyrant's neck must yet be bent,
  The price of blood be told:
The city yet must hear the roar
  Of Baird's avenging guns,
And see him stand with lifted hand
  By Tippoo Sahib's sons.

The lads were bonny, the lads were young,
  But he claimed a pitiless debt;
Life and death in the balance hung,
  They watched it swing and set.
They saw him search with sombre eyes,
  They knew the place he sought;
They saw him feel for the hilted steel,
  They bowed before his thought.

But he—he saw the prison there
  In the old quivering heat,
Where merry hearts had met despair
  And died without defeat;
Where feeble hands had raised the cup
  For feebler lips to drain,
And one had worn with smiling scorn
  His double load of pain.

"The sleep that Tippoo Sahib sleeps
  Hears not the voice of man;
The faith that Tippoo Sahib keeps
  No earthly judge may scan;
For all the wrong your father wrought
  Your father's sons are free;
Where Lucas lay no tongue shall say
  That Mercy bound not me."

A Ballad of John Nicholson

It fell in the year of Mutiny,
  At darkest of the night,
John Nicholson by Jalándhar came,
  On his way to Delhi fight.

And as he by Jalándhar came,
  He thought what he must do,
And he sent to the Rajah fair greeting,
  To try if he were true.

"God grant your Highness length of days,
  And friends when need shall be;
And I pray you send your Captains hither,
  That they may speak with me."

On the morrow through Jalándhar town
  The Captains rode in state;
They came to the house of John Nicholson,
  And stood before the gate.

The chief of them was Mehtab Singh,
  He was both proud and sly;
His turban gleamed with rubies red,
  He held his chin full high.

He marked his fellows how they put
  Their shoes from off their feet;
"Now wherefore make ye such ado
  These fallen lords to greet?

"They have ruled us for a hundred years,
  In truth I know not how,
But though they be fain of mastery
  They dare not claim it now."

Right haughtily before them all
  The durbar hall he trod,
With rubies red his turban gleamed,
  His feet with pride were shod.

They had not been an hour together,
  A scanty hour or so,
When Mehtab Singh rose in his place
  And turned about to go.

Then swiftly came John Nicholson
  Between the door and him,
With anger smouldering in his eyes,
  That made the rubies dim.

"You are over-hasty, Mehtab Singh," —-
  Oh, but his voice was low!
He held his wrath with a curb of iron
  That furrowed cheek and brow.

"You are overhasty, Mehtab Singh,
  When that the rest are gone,
I have a word that may not wait
  To speak with you alone."

The Captains passed in silence forth
  And stood the door behind;
To go before the game was played
  Be sure they had no mind.

But there within John Nicholson
  Turned him on Mehtab Singh,
"So long as the soul is in my body
  You shall not do this thing.

"Have ye served us for a hundred years
  And yet ye know not why?
We brook no doubt of our mastery,
  We rule until we die.

"Were I the one last Englishman
  Drawing the breath of life,
And you the master-rebel of all
  That stir this land to strife—-

"Were I," he said, "but a Corporal,
  And you a Rajput King,
So long as the soul was in my body
  You should not do this thing.

"Take off, take off, those shoes of pride,
  Carry them whence they came;
Your Captains saw your insolence,
  And they shall see your shame."

When Mehtab Singh came to the door
  His shoes they burned his hand,
For there in long and silent lines
  He saw the Captains stand.

When Mehtab Singh rode from the gate
  His chin was on his breast:
The Captains said, "When the strong command
  Obedience is best."

The Guides at Cabul

(1879)

Sons of the Island race, wherever ye dwell,
  Who speak of your fathers' battles with lips that burn,
The deed of an alien legion hear me tell,
  And think not shame from the hearts ye tamed to learn,
  When succour shall fail and the tide for a season turn,
To fight with joyful courage, a passionate pride,
To die at last as the Guides of Cabul died.

For a handful of seventy men in a barrack of mud,
  Foodless, waterless, dwindling one by one,
Answered a thousand yelling for English blood
  With stormy volleys that swept them gunner from gun,
  And charge on charge in the glare of the Afghan sun,
Till the walls were shattered wherein they couched at bay,
And dead or dying half of the seventy lay.

Twice they had taken the cannon that wrecked their hold,
  Twice toiled in vain to drag it back,
Thrice they toiled, and alone, wary and bold,
  Whirling a hurricane sword to scatter the rack,
  Hamilton, last of the English, covered their track.
"Never give in!" he cried, and he heard them shout,
And grappled with death as a man that knows not doubt.

And the Guides looked down from their smouldering barrack again,
  And behold, a banner of truce, and a voice that spoke:
"Come, for we know that the English all are slain,
  We keep no feud with men of a kindred folk;
  Rejoice with us to be free of the conqueror's yolk."
Silence fell for a moment, then was heard
A sound of laughter and scorn, and an answering word.

"Is it we or the lords we serve who have earned this wrong,
  That ye call us to flinch from the battle they bade us fight?
We that live—do ye doubt that our hands are strong?
  They that are fallen—ye know that their blood was bright!
  Think ye the Guides will barter for lust of the light
The pride of an ancient people in warfare bred,
Honour of comrades living, and faith to the dead?"

Then the joy that spurs the warrior's heart
  To the last thundering gallop and sheer leap
Came on the men of the Guides: they flung apart
  The doors not all their valour could longer keep;
  They dressed their slender line; they breathed deep,
And with never a foot lagging or head bent
To the clash and clamour and dust of death they went.

The Gay Gordons

(Dargai, October 20, 1897)

Whos for the Gathering, who's for the Fair?
   (Gay goes the Gordon to a fight)
The bravest of the brave are at deadlock there,
   (Highlanders! march! by the right!)
There are bullets by the hundred buzzing in the air,
There are bonny lads lying on the hillside bare;
But the Gordons know what the Gordons dare
  When they hear the pipers playing!

The happiest English heart today
   (Gay goes the Gordon to a fight)
Is the heart of the Colonel, hide it as he may;
   (Steady there! steady on the right!)
He sees his work and he sees his way,
He knows his time and the word to say,
And he's thinking of the tune that the Gordons play
  When he sets the pipers playing.

Rising, roaring, rushing like the tide,
   (Gay goes the Gordon to a fight)
They're up through the fire-zone, not be be denied;
   (Bayonets! and charge! by the right!)
Thirty bullets straight where the rest went wide,
And thirty lads are lying on the bare hillside;
But they passed in the hour of the Gordons' pride,
  To the skirl of the pipers' playing.

He Fell Among Thieves

"Ye have robbed," said he, "ye have slaughtered and made an end,
  Take your ill-got plunder, and bury the dead:
What will ye more of your guest and sometime friend?"
  "Blood for our blood," they said.

He laughed: "If one may settle the score for five,
  I am ready; but let the reckoning stand til day:
I have loved the sunlight as dearly as any alive."
  "You shall die at dawn," said they.

He flung his empty revolver down the slope,
  He climbed alone to the Eastward edge of the trees;
All night long in a dream untroubled of hope
  He brooded, clasping his knees.

He did not hear the monotonous roar that fills
  The ravine where the Yassin river sullenly flows;
He did not see the starlight on the Laspur hills,
  Or the far Afghan snows.

He saw the April noon on his books aglow,
  The wistaria trailing in at the window wide;
He heard his father's voice from the terrace below
  Calling him down to ride.

He saw the gray little church across the park,
  The mounds that hid the loved and honoured dead;
The Norman arch, the chancel softly dark,
  The brasses black and red.

He saw the School Close, sunny and green,
  The runner beside him, the stand by the parapet wall,
The distant tape, and the crowd roaring between,
  His own name over all.

He saw the dark wainscot and timbered roof,
  The long tables, and the faces merry and keen;
The College Eight and their trainer dining aloof,
  The Dons on the daïs serene.

He watched the liner's stem ploughing the foam,
  He felt her trembling speed and the thrash of her screw;
He heard the passengers' voices talking of home,
  He saw the flag she flew.

And now it was dawn. He rose strong on his feet,
  And strode to his ruined camp below the wood;
He drank the breath of the morning cool and sweet:
  His murderers round him stood.

Light on the Laspur hills was broadening fast,
  The blood-red snow-peaks chilled to dazzling white:
He turned, and saw the golden circle at last,
  Cut by the Eastern height.

"O glorious Life, Who dwellest in earth and sun,
  I have lived, I praise and adore Thee."
                    A sword swept.
Over the pass the voices one by one
  Faded, and the hill slept.

Ionicus

With failing feet and shoulders bowed
  Beneath the weight of happier days,
He lagged among the heedless crowd,
  Or crept along suburban ways.
But still through all his heart was young,
  His mood a joy that nought could mar,
A courage, a pride, a rapture, sprung
  Of the strength and splendour of England's war.

From ill-requited toil he turned
  To ride with Picton and with Pack,
Among his grammars inly burned
  To storm the Afghan mountain-track.
When midnight chimed, before Quebec
  He watched with Wolfe till the morning star;
At noon he saw from *Victory's* deck
  The sweep and splendour of England's war.

Beyond the book his teaching sped,
  He left on whom he taught the trace
Of kinship with the deathless dead,
  And faith in all the Island Race.
He passed: his life a tangle seemed,
  His age from fame and power was far;
But his heart was night to the end, and dreamed
  Of the sound and splendour of England's war.

The Non-Combatant

Among a race high-handed, strong of heart,
Sea-rovers, conquerors, builders in the waste,
He had his birth; a nature too complete,
Eager and doubtful, no man's soldier sworn
And no man's chosen captain; born to fail,
A name without an echo: yet he too
Within the cloister of his narrow days
Fulfilled the ancestral rites, and kept alive
The eternal fire; it may be, not in vain;
For out of those who dropped a downward glance
Upon the weakling huddled at his prayers,
Perchance some looked beyond him, and then first
Beheld the glory, and what shrine it filled,
And to what Spirit sacred: or perchance
Some heard him chanting, though but to himself,
The old heroic names: and went their way:
And hummed his music on the march to death.

Clifton Chapel

This is the Chapel: here, my son,
  Your father thought the thoughts of youth,
And heard the words that one by one
  The touch of Life has turned to truth.
Here in a day that is not far,
  You too may speak with noble ghosts
Of manhood and the vows of war
  You made before the Lord of Hosts.

To set the cause above renown,
  To love the game beyond the prize,
To honour, while you strike him down,
  The foe that comes with fearless eyes;
To count the life of battle good,
  And dear the land that gave you birth,
And dearer yet the brotherhood
  That binds the brave of all the earth—-

My son, the oath is yours: the end
  Is His, Who built the world of strife,
Who gave His children Pain for friend,
  And Death for surest hope of life.
To-day and here the fight's begun,
  Of the great fellowship you're free;
Henceforth the School and you are one,
  And what You are, the race shall be.

God send you fortune: yet be sure,
  Among the lights that gleam and pass,
You'll live to follow none more pure
  Than that which glows on yonder brass:
"Qui procul hinc," the legend's writ,—-
  The frontier-grave is far away—-
"Qui ante diem periit:
  Sed miles, sed pro patriâ."

Vitaï Lampada

There's a breathless hush in the Close to-night—-
  Ten to make and the match to win—-
A bumping pitch and a blinding light,
  An hour to play and the last man in.
And it's not for the sake of a ribboned coat,
  Or the selfish hope of a season's fame,
But his Captain's hand on his shoulder smote—-
  "Play up! play up! and play the game!"

The sand of the desert is sodden red,—-
  Red with the wreck of a square that broke;—-
The Gatling's jammed and the colonel dead,
  And the regiment blind with dust and smoke.
The river of death has brimmed his banks,
  And England's far, and Honour a name,
But the voice of schoolboy rallies the ranks,
  "Play up! play up! and play the game!"

This is the word that year by year,
  While in her place the School is set,
Every one of her sons must hear,
  And none that hears it dare forget.
This they all with a joyful mind
  Bear through life like a torch in flame,
And falling fling to the host behind—-
  "Play up! play up! and play the game!"

The Vigil

England! where the sacred flame
  Burns before the inmost shrine,
Where the lips that love thy name
  Consecrate their hopes and thine,
Where the banners of thy dead
Weave their shadows overhead,
Watch beside thine arms to-night,
Pray that God defend the Right.

Think that when to-morrow comes
  War shall claim command of all,
Thou must hear the roll of drums,
  Thou must hear the trumpet's call.
Now, before they silence ruth,
Commune with the voice of truth;
England! on thy knees to-night
Pray that God defend the Right.

Hast thou counted up the cost,
  What to foeman, what to friend?
Glory sought is Honour lost,
  How should this be knighthood's end?
Know'st thou what is Hatred's meed?
What the surest gain of greed?
England! wilt thou dare to-night
Pray that God defend the Right.

Single-hearted, unafraid,
  Hither all thy heroes came,
On this altar's steps were laid
  Gordon's life and Outram's fame.
England! if thy will be yet
By their great example set,
Here beside thine arms to-night
Pray that God defend the Right.

So shalt thou when morning comes
  Rise to conquer or to fall,
Joyful hear the rolling drums,
  Joyful hear the trumpets call,

Then let Memory tell thy heart:
"England! what thou wert, thou art!"
Gird thee with thine ancient might,
Forth! and God defend the Right!

The Sailing Of The Long-Ships

(October, 1899)

They saw the cables loosened, they saw the gangways cleared,
They heard the women weeping, they heard the men that cheered;
Far off, far off, the tumult faded and died away,
And all alone the sea-wind came singing up the Bay.

"I came by Cape St. Vincent, I came by Trafalgar,
I swept from Torres Vedras to golden Vigo Bar,
I saw the beacons blazing that fired the world with light
When down their ancient highway your fathers passed to fight.

"O race of tireless fighters, flushed with a youth renewed,
Right well the wars of Freedom befit the Sea-kings' brood;
Yet as ye go forget not the fame of yonder shore,
The fame ye owe your fathers and the old time before.

"Long-suffering were the Sea-kings, they were not swift to kill,
But when the sands had fallen they waited no man's will;
Though all the world forbade them, they counted not nor cared,
They weighed not help or hindrance, they did the thing they dared.

"The Sea-kings loved not boasting, they cursed not him that cursed,
They honoured all men duly, and him that faced them, first;
They strove and knew not hatred, they smote and toiled to save,
They tended whom they vanquished, they praised the fallen brave.

"Their fame's on Torres Vedras, their fame's on Vigo Bar,
Far-flashed to Cape St. Vincent it burns from Trafalgar;
Mark as ye go the beacons that woke the world with light
When down their ancient highway your fathers passed to fight."

Waggon Hill

Drake in the North Sea grimly prowling,
  Treading his dear *Revenge's* deck,
Watched, with the sea-dogs round him growling,
  Galleons drifting wreck by wreck.
  "Fetter and Faith for England's neck,
  Faggot and Father, Saint and chain, —-
Yonder the Devil and all go howling,
  Devon, O Devon, in wind and rain!

Drake at the last off Nombre lying,
  Knowing the night that toward him crept,
Gave to the sea-dogs round him crying,
  This for a sign before he slept: —-
  "Pride of the West! What Devon hath kept
  Devon shall keep on tide or main;
Call to the storm and drive them flying,
  Devon, O Devon, in wind and rain!"

Valour of England gaunt and whitening,
  Far in a South land brought to bay,
Locked in a death-grip all day tightening,
  Waited the end in twilight gray.
  Battle and storm and the sea-dog's way!
  Drake from his long rest turned again,
Victory lit thy steel with lightning,
  Devon, o Devon, in wind and rain!

The Volunteer

"He leapt to arms unbidden,
  Unneeded, over-bold;
His face by earth is hidden,
  His heart in earth is cold.

"Curse on the reckless daring
  That could not wait the call,
The proud fantastic bearing
  That would be first to fall!"

O tears of human passion,
  Blur not the image true;
This was not folly's fashion,
  This was the man we knew.

The Only Son

O Bitter wind toward the sunset blowing,
  What of the dales to-night?
In yonder gray old hall what fires are glowing,
  What ring of festal light?

    "In the great window as the day was dwindling
      I saw an old man stand;
    His head was proudly held and his eyes kindling,
      But the list shook in his hand."

O wind of twilight, was there no word uttered,
  No sound of joy or wail?
"'A great fight and a good death,' he muttered;
  'Trust him, he would not fail.'"

What of the chamber dark where she was lying;
  For whom all life is done?
"Within her heart she rocks a dead child, crying
  'My son, my ltttle son.'"

The Grenadier's Good-Bye

"When Lieutenant Murray fell, the only words he spoke were,
'Forward, Grenadiers!'"—-Press Telegram.

Here they halted, here once more
  Hand from hand was rent;
Here his voice above the roar
  Rang, and on they went.
Yonder out of sight they crossed,
  Yonder died the cheers;
One word lives where all is lost—-
  "Forward, Grenadiers!"

This alone he asked of fame,
  This alone of pride;
Still with this he faced the flame,
  Answered Death, and died.
Crest of battle sunward tossed,
  Song of the marching years,
This shall live though all be lost—-
  "Forward, Grenadiers!"

The Schoolfellow

Our game was his but yesteryear;
  We wished him back; we could not know
The self-same hour we missed him here
  He led the line that broke the foe.

Blood-red behind our guarded posts
  Sank as of old and dying day;
The battle ceased; the mingled hosts
  Weary and cheery went their way:

"To-morrow well may bring," we said,
  "As fair a fight, as clear a sun."
Dear lad, before the world was sped,
  For evermore thy goal was won.

On Spion Kop

Foremost of all on battle's fiery steep
  Here VERTUE fell, and here he sleeps his sleep.*
A fairer name no Roman ever gave
  To stand sole monument on Valour's grave.

* Major N. H. Vertue, of the Buffs, Brigade-Major to General Woodgate, was buried where he fell, on the edge of Spion Kop, in front of the British position.

The School At War

All night before the brink of death
  In fitful sleep the army lay,
For through the dream that stilled their breath
  Too gauntly glared the coming day.

But we, within whose blood there leaps
  The fulness of a life as wide
As Avon's water where he sweeps
  Seaward at last with Severn's tide,

We heard beyond the desert night
  The murmur of the fields we knew,
And our swift souls with one delight
  Like homing swallows Northward flew.

We played again the immortal games,
  And grappled with the fierce old friends,
And cheered the dead undying names,
  And sang the song that never ends;

Till, when the hard, familiar bell
  Told that the summer night was late,
Where long ago we said farewell
  We said farewell by the old gate.

"O Captains unforgot," they cried,
  "Come you again or come no more,
Across the world you keep the pride,
  Across the world we mark the score."

By The Hearth-Stone

By the hearth-stone
She sits alone,
  The long night bearing:
With eyes that gleam
Into the dream
  Of the firelight staring.

Low and more low
The dying glow
  Burns in the embers;
She nothing heeds
And nothing needs—-
  Only remembers.

Peace

No more to watch by Night's eternal shore,
  With England's chivalry at dawn to ride;
No more defeat, faith, victory —-O! no more
  A cause on earth for which we might have died.

April On Waggon Hill

Lad, and can you rest now,
  There beneath your hill!
Your hands are on your breast now,
  But is your heart so still?
'Twas the right death to die, lad,
  A gift without regret,
But unless truth's a lie, lad,
  You dream of Devon yet.

Ay, ay, the year's awaking,
  The fire's among the ling,
The beechen hedge is breaking,
  The curlew's on the wing;
Primroses are out, lad,
  On the high banks of Lee,
And the sun stirs the trout, lad;
  From Brendon to the sea.

I know what's in your heart, lad,—-
  The mare he used to hunt—-
And her blue market-cart, lad,
  With posies tied in front—-
We miss them from the moor road,
  They're getting old to roam,
The road they're on's a sure road
  And nearer, lad, to home.

Your name, the name they cherish?
  'Twill fade, lad, 'tis true:
But stone and all may perish
  With little loss to you.
While fame's fame you're Devon, lad,
  The Glory of the West;
Till the roll's called in heaven, lad,
  You may well take your rest.

Commemoration

I sat by the granite pillar, and sunlight fell
  Where the sunlight fell of old,
And the hour was the hour my heart remembered well,
  And the sermon rolled and rolled
As it used to roll when the place was still unhaunted,
And the strangest tale in the world was still untold.

And I knew that of all this rushing of urgent sound
  That I so clearly heard,
The green young forest of saplings clustered round
  Was heeding not one word:
Their heads were bowed in a still serried patience
Such as an angel's breath could never have stirred.

For some were already away to the hazardous pitch,
  Or lining the parapet wall,
And some were in glorious battle, or great and rich,
  Or throned in a college hall:
And among the rest was one like my own young phantom,
Dreaming for ever beyond my utmost call.

"O Youth," the preacher was crying, "deem not thou
  Thy life is thine alone;
Thou bearest the will of the ages, seeing how
  They built thee bone by bone,
And within thy blood the Great Age sleeps sepulchred
Till thou and thine shall roll away the stone.

"Therefore the days are coming when thou shalt burn
  With passion whitely hot;
Rest shall be rest no more; thy feet shall spurn
  All that thy hand hath got;
And One that is stronger shall gird thee, and lead thee swiftly
Whither, O heart of Youth, thou wouldest not."

And the School passed; and I saw the living and dead
  Set in their seats again,
And I longed to hear them speak of the word that was said,
  But I knew that I longed in vain.
And they stretched forth their hands, and the wind of the spirit took them
Lightly as drifted leaves on an endless plain.

The Echo

Of A Ballad Sung By H. Plunket Greene To His Old School

Twice three hundred boys were we,
    Long ago, long ago,
Where the Downs look out to the Severn Sea.
    Clifton for aye!
We held by the game and hailed the team,
For many could play where few could dream.
    City of Song shall stand alway.

Some were for profit and some for pride,
    Long ago, long ago,
Some for the flag they lived and died.
    Clifton for aye!
The work of the world must still be done,
And minds are many though truth be one.
    City of Song shall stand alway.

But a lad there was to his fellows sang,
    Long ago, long ago,
And soon the world to his music rang.
    Clifton for aye!
Follow your Captains, crown your Kings,
But what will ye give to the lad that sings?
    City of Song shall stand alway.

For the voice ye hear is the voice of home,
    Long ago, long ago,
And the voice of Youth with the world to roam.
    Clifton for aye!
The voice of passion and human tears,
And the voice of the vision that lights the years.
    City of Song shall stand alway.

The Best School of All

It's good to see the school we knew,
  The land of youth and dream.
To greet again the rule we knew
  Before we took the stream:
Though long we've missed the sight of her,
  Our hearts may not forget;
We've lost the old delight of her,
  We keep her honour yet.

  We'll honour yet the school we knew,
    The best school of all:
  We'll honour yet the rule we knew,
    Till the last bell call.
  For working days or holidays,
    And glad or melancholy days,
  They were great days and jolly days
    At the best school of all.

The stars and sounding vanities
  That half the crowd bewitch,
What are they but inanities
  To him that treads the pitch?
And where's the welth I'm wondering,
  Could buy the cheers that roll
When the last charge goes thundering
  Towards the twilight goal?

Then men that tanned the hide of us,
  Our daily foes and friends,
They shall not lose their pride of us,
  Howe'er the journey ends.
Their voice to us who sing of it,
  No more its message bears,
But the round world shall ring of it,
  And all we are be theirs.

To speak of fame a venture is,
  There's little here can bide,
But we may face the centuries,
  And dare the deepending tide:

for though the dust that's part of us,
  To dust again be gone,
Yet here shall beat the heart of us—-
  The school we handed on!

  We'll honour yet the school we knew,
    The best school of all:
  We'll honour yet the rule we knew,
    Till the last bell call.
  For working days or holidays,
    And glad or melancholy days,
  They were great days and jolly days
    At the best school of all.

England

Praise thou with praise unending,
  The Master of the Wine;
To all their portions sending
  Himself he mingled thine:

The sea-born flush of morning,
  The sea-born hush of night,
The East wind comfort scorning,
  And the North wind driving right:

The world for gain and giving,
  The game for man and boy,
The life that joys in living,
  The faith that lives in joy.

Victoria Regina

(June 21st, 1897*)

A thousand years by sea and land
  Our race hath served the island kings,
But not by custom's dull command
  To-day with song her Empire rings:

Not all the glories of her birth,
  Her armed renown and ancient throne,
Could make her less the child of earth
  Or give her hopes beyond our own:

But stayed on faith more sternly proved
  And pride than ours more pure and deep,
She loves the land our fathers loved
  And keeps the fame our sons shall keep.

* These lines, with music by Dr. Lloyd, formed part of the Cycle of Song offered to Queen Victoria, of blessed and glorious memory, in celebration of her second Jubilee.

The King Of England

(June 24th, 1902)

In that eclipse of noon when joy was hushed
　Like the bird's song beneath unnatural night,
And Terror's footfall in the darkness crushed
　The rose imperial of our delight,
Then, even then, though no man cried "He comes,"
　And no man turned to greet him passing there,
　With phantom heralds challenging renown
　　And silent-throbbing drums
　I saw the King of England, hale and fair,
　　Ride out with a great train through London town.

Unarmed he rode, but in his ruddy shield
　The lions bore the dint of many a lance,
And up and down his mantle's azure field
　Were strewn the lilies plucked in famous France.
Before him went with banner floating wide
　The yeoman breed that served his honour best,
　And mixed with these his knights of noble blood;
　　But in the place of pride
　His admirals in billowy lines abreast
　　Convoyed him close like galleons on the flood.

Full of a strength unbroken showed his face
　And his brow calm with youth's unclouded dawn,
But round his lips were lines of tenderer grace
　Such as no hand but Time's hath ever drawn.
Surely he knew his glory had no part
　In dull decay, nor unto Death must bend,
　Yet surely too of lengthening shadows dreamed
　　With sunset in his heart,
　So brief his beauty now, so near the end,
　　And now so old and so immortal seemed.

O King among the living, these shall hail
　Sons of thy dust that shall inherit thee:
O King of men that die, though we must fail
　Thy life is breathed from thy triumphant sea.
O man that servest men by right of birth,

Our hearts' content thy heart shall also keep,
  Thou too with us shalt one day lay thee down
   In our dear native earth,
Full sure the King of England, while we sleep,
  For ever rides abroad, through London town.

The Nile

Out of the unknown South,
Through the dark lands of drouth,
  Far wanders ancient Nile in slumber gliding:
Clear-mirrored in his dream
The deeds that haunt his stream
  Flash out and fade like stars in midnight sliding.
Long since, before the life of man
  Rose from among the lives that creep,
With Time's own tide began
  That still mysterious sleep,
  Only to cease when Time shall reach the eternal deep.

From out his vision vast
The early gods have passed,
  They waned and perished with the faith that made them;
The long phantasmal line
Of Pharaohs crowned divine
  Are dust among the dust that once obeyed them.
Their land is one mute burial mound,
  Save when across the drifted years
Some chant of hollow sound,
  Some triumph blent with tears,
  From Memnon's lips at dawn wakens the desert meres.

O Nile, and can it be
No memory dwells with thee
  Of Grecian lore and the sweet Grecian singer?
The legions' iron tramp,
The Goths' wide-wandering camp,
  Had these no fame that by thy shore might linger?
Nay, then must all be lost indeed,
  Lost too the swift pursuing might
That cleft with passionate speed
  Aboukir's tranquil night,
  And shattered in mid-swoop the great world-eagle's flight.

Yet have there been on earth
Spirits of starry birth,
  Whose splendour rushed to no eternal setting:
They over all endure,

Their course through all is sure,
  The dark world's light is still of their begetting.
Though the long past forgotten lies,
  Nile! in thy dream remember him,
Whose like no more shall rise
  Above our twilight's rim,
  Until the immortal dawn shall make all glories dim.

For this man was not great
By gold or kingly state,
  Or the bright sword, or knowledge of earth's wonder;
But more than all his race
He saw life face to face,
  And heard the still small voice above the thunder.
O river, while thy waters roll
  By yonder vast deserted tomb,
There, where so clear a soul
  So shone through gathering doom,
  Thou and thy land shall keep the tale of lost Khartoum.

Sráhmandázi*

Deep embowered beside the forest river,
  Where the flame of sunset only falls,
Lapped in silence lies the House of Dying,
  House of them to whom the twilight calls.

There within when day was near to ending,
  By her lord a woman young and strong,
By his chief a songman old and stricken
  Watched together till the hour of song.

"O my songman, now the bow is broken,
  Now the arrows one by one are sped,
Sing to me the song of Sráhmandázi,
  Sráhmandázi, home of all the dead."

Then the songman, flinging wide his songnet,
  On the last token laid his master's hand,
While he sang the song of Sráhmandázi,
  None but dying men can understand.

"Yonder sun that fierce and fiery-hearted
  Marches down the sky to vanish soon,
At the self-same hour in Sráhmandázi
  Rises pallid like the rainy moon.

"There he sees the heroes by their river,
  Where the great fish daily upward swim;
Yet they are but shadows hunting shadows,
  Phantom fish in waters drear and dim.

"There he sees the kings among their headmen,
  Women weaving, children playing games;
Yet they are but shadows ruling shadows,
  Phantom folk with dim forgotten names.

"Bid farewell to all that most thou lovest,
  Tell thy heart thy living life is done;
All the days and deeds of Sráhmandázi
  Are not worth an hour of yonder sun.

Dreamily the chief from out the songnet
  Drew his hand and touched the woman's head:
"Know they not, then, love in Sráhmandázi?
  Has a king no bride among the dead?"

Then the songman answered, "O my master,
  Love they know, but none may learn it there;
Only souls that reach that land together
  Keep their troth and find the twilight fair.

"Thou art still a king, and at thy passing
  By thy latest word must all abide:
If thou willest, here am I, thy songman;
  If thou lovest, here is she, thy bride."

Hushed and dreamy lay the House of Dying,
  Dreamily the sunlight upward failed,
Dreamily the chief on eyes that loved him
  Looked with eyes the coming twilight veiled.

Then he cried, "My songman, I am passing;
  Let her live, her life is but begun;
All the days and nights of Sráhmandázi
  Are not worth an hour of yonder sun."

Yet, when there within the House of Dying
  The last silence held the sunset air,
Not alone he came to Sráhmandázi,
  Not alone she found the twilight fair:

While the songman, far beneath the forest
  Sang of Srahmandazi all night through,
"Lovely be thy name, O Land of shadows,
  Land of meeting, Land of all the true!"

* This ballad is founded on materials given to the author by the late
Miss Mary Kingsley on her return from her last visit to the Bantu
peoples of West Africa.

Outward Bound

Dear Earth, near Earth, the clay that made us men,
  The land we sowed,
  The hearth that glowed—-
  O Mother, must we bid farewell to thee?
Fast dawns the last dawn, and what shall comfort then
  The lonely hearts that roam the outer sea?

Gray wakes the daybreak, the shivering sails are set,
  To misty deeps
  The channel sweeps—-
  O Mother, think on us who think on thee!
Earth-home, birth-home, with love remember yet
  The sons in exile on the eternal sea.

Hope The Hornblower

"Hark ye, hark to the winding horn;
Sluggards, awake, and front the morn!
Hark ye, hark to the winding horn;
  The sun's on meadow and mill.
Follow me, hearts that love the chase;
Follow me, feet that keep the pace:
Stirrup to stirrup we ride, we ride,
  We ride by moor and hill."

Huntsman, huntsman, whither away?
What is the quarry afoot to-day?
Huntsman, huntsman, whither away,
  And what the game ye kill?
Is it the deer, that men may dine?
Is it the wolf that tears the kine?
What is the race ye ride, ye ride,
  Ye ride by moor and hill?

"Ask not yet till the day be dead
What is the game that's forward fled,
Ask not yet till the day be dead
  The game we follow still.
An echo it may be, floating past;
A shadow it may be, fading fast:
Shadow or echo, we ride, we ride,
  We ride by moor and hill"

O Pulchritudo

O Saint whose thousand shrines our feet have trod
  And our eyes loved thy lamp's eternal beam,
Dim earthly radiance of the Unknown God,
  Hope of the darkness, light of them that dream,
Far off, far off and faint, O glimmer on
Till we thy pilgrims from the road are gone.

O Word whose meaning every sense hath sought,
  Voice of the teeming field and grassy mound,
Deep-whispering fountain of the wells of thought,
  Will of the wind and soul of all sweet sound,
Far off, far off and faint, O murmur on
Till we thy pilgrims from the road are gone.

In July

His beauty bore no token,
  No sign our gladness shook;
With tender strength unbroken
  The hand of Life he took:
But the summer flowers were falling,
  Falling and fading away,
And mother birds were calling,
    Crying and calling
  For their loves that would not stay.

He knew not Autumn's chillness,
  Nor Winter's wind nor Spring's.
He lived with Summer's stillness
  And sun and sunlit things:
But when the dusk was falling
  He went the shadowy way,
And one more heart is calling,
    Crying and calling
  For the love that would not stay.

From Generation To Generation

O Son of mine, when dusk shall find thee bending
  Between a gravestone and a cradle's head —-
Between the love whose name is loss unending
  And the young love whose thoughts are liker dread, —-
Thou too shalt groan at heart that all thy spending
  Cannot repay the dead, the hungry dead.

When I Remember

When I remember that the day will come
  For this our love to quit his land of birth,
  And bid farewell to all the ways of earth
With lips that must for evermore be dumb,

Then creep I silent from the stirring hum,
  And shut away the music and the mirth,
  And reckon up what may be left of worth
When hearts are cold and love's own body numb.

Something there must be that I know not here,
Or know too dimly through the symbol dear;
  Some touch, some beauty, only guessed by this —-
If He that made us loves, it shall replace,
Beloved, even the vision of thy face
  And deep communion of thine inmost kiss.

Rondel*

Though I wander far-off ways,
  Dearest, never doubt thou me:

Mine is not the love that strays,
Though I wander far-off ways:

Faithfully for all my days
  I have vowed myself to thee:
Though I wander far-off ways,
  Dearest, never doubt thou me.

* This and the two following pieces are from the French of
Wenceslas, Duke of Brabant and Luxembourg, who died in 1384.

Rondel

Long ago to thee I gave
Body, soul, and all I have—-
  Nothing in the world I keep:

All that in return I crave
Is that thou accept the slave
Long ago to thee I gave—-
Body, soul, and all I have.

Had I more to share or save,
I would give as give the brave,
  Stooping not to part the heap;
Long ago to thee I gave
Body, soul, and all I have—-
  Nothing in the world I keep.

Balade

I cannot tell, of twain beneath this bond,
Which one in grief the other goes beyond,—-
Narcissus, who to end the pain he bore
Died of the love that could not help him more;
Or I, that pine because I cannot see
The lady who is queen and love to me.

Nay—for Narcissus, in the forest pond
Seeing his image, made entreaty fond,
"Beloved, comfort on my longing pour":
So for a while he soothed his passion sore;
So cannot I, for all too far is she—-
The lady who is queen and love to me.

But since that I have Love's true colours donned,
I in his service will not now despond,
For in extremes Love yet can all restore:
So till her beauty walks the world no more
All day remembered in my hope shall be
The lady who is queen and love to me.

The Last Word

Before the April night was late
A rider came to the castle gate;
A rider breathing human breath,
But the words he spoke were the words of Death.

"Greet you well from the King our lord,
He marches hot for the eastward ford;
Living or dying, all or one,
Ye must keep the ford till the race be run.

Sir Alain rose with lips that smiled,
He kissed his wife, he kissed his child:
Before the April night was late
Sir Alain rode from the castle gate.

He called his men-at-arms by name,
But one there was uncalled that came:
He bade his troop behind him ride,
But there was one that rode beside.

  "Why will you spur so fast to die?
  Be wiser ere the night go by.
  A message late is a message lost;
  For all your haste the foe had crossed.

  "Are men such small unmeaning things
  To strew the board of smiling Kings?
  With life and death they play their game,
  And life or death, the end's the same."

Softly the April air above
Rustled the woodland homes of love:
Softly the April air below
Carried the dream of buds that blow.

  "Is he that bears a warrior's fame
  To shun the pointless stroke of shame?
  Will he that propped a trembling throne
  Not stand for right when right's his own?

"Your oath on the four gospels sworn?
What oath can bind resolves unborn?
You lose that far eternal life?
Is it yours to lose? Is it child and wife?

But now beyond the pathway's bend,
Sir Alain saw the forest end,
And winding wide beneath the hill,
The glassy river lone and still.

And now he saw with lifted eyes
The East like a great chancel rise,
And deep through all his senses drawn,
Received the sacred wine of dawn.

He set his face to the stream below,
He drew his axe from the saddle bow:
"Farewell, Messire, the night is sped;
There lies the ford, when all is said"

The Viking's Song

When I thy lover first
  Shook out my canvas free
And like a pirate burst
  Into that dreaming sea,
The land knew no such thirst
  As then tormented me.

Now when at eve returned
  I near that shore divine,
Where once but watch-fires burned
  I see thy beacon shine,
And know the land hath learned
  Desire that welcomes mine.

The Sufi In The City

I.

When late I watched the arrows of the sleet
Against the windows of the Tavern beat,
  I heard a Rose that murmured from her Pot:
"Why trudge thy fellows yonder in the Street?

II.

"Before the phantom of False Morning dies,
Choked in the bitter Net that binds the skies,
  Their feet, bemired with Yesterday, set out
For the dark alleys where To-morrow lies.

III.

"Think you, when all their petals they have bruised,
And all the fragrances of Life confused,
  That Night with sweeter rest will comfort these
Than us, who still within the Garden mused?

IV.

"Think you the Gold they fight for all day long
Is worth the frugal Peace their clamours wrong?
  Their Titles, and the Name they toil to build—-
Will they outlast the echoes of our Song?"

V.

O Sons of Omar, what shall be the close
Seek not to know, for no man living knows:
  But while within your hands the Wine is set
Drink ye—to Omar and the Dreaming Rose!

Yattendon

Among the woods and tillage
  That fringe the topmost downs,
All lonely lies the village,
  Far off from seas and towns.
Yet when her own folk slumbered
  I heard within her street
Murmur of men unnumbered
  And march of myriad feet.

For all she lies so lonely,
  Far off from towns and seas,
The village holds not only
  The roofs beneath her trees:
While Life is sweet and tragic
  And Death is veiled and dumb,
Hither, by singer's magic,
  The pilgrim world must come.

Among The Tombs

She is a lady fair and wise,
  Her heart her counsel keeps,
And well she knows of time that flies
  And tide that onward sweeps;
But still she sits with restless eyes
  Where Memory sleeps—-
  Where Memory sleeps.

Ye that have heard the whispering dead
  In every wind that creeps,
Or felt the stir that strains the lead
  Beneath the mounded heaps,
Tread softly, ah! more softly tread
  Where Memory sleeps—-
  Where Memory sleeps.

A Sower

With sanguine looks
  And rolling walk
Among the rooks
  He loved to stalk,

While on the land
  With gusty laugh
From a full hand
  He scattered chaff.

Now that within
  His spirit sleeps
A harvest thin
  The sickle reaps;

But the dumb fields
  Desire his tread,
And no earth yields
  A wheat more red.

A Song Of Exmoor

The Forest above and the Combe below,
  On a bright September morn!
He's the soul of a clod who thanks not God
  That ever his body was born!
So hurry along, the stag's afoot,
  The Master's up and away!
Halloo! Halloo! we'll follow it through
From Bratton to Porlock Bay!

  So hurry along, the stag's afoot,
    The Master's up and away!
  Halloo! Halloo! we'll follow it through
    From Bratton to Porlock Bay!

Hark to the tufters' challenge true,
  'Tis a note that the red-deer knows!
His courage awakes, his covert he breaks,
  And up for the moor he goes!
He's all his rights and seven on top,
  His eye's the eye of a king,
And he'll beggar the pride of some that ride
  Before he leaves the ling!

Here comes Antony bringing the pack,
  Steady! he's laying them on!
By the sound of their chime you may tell that it's time
  To harden your heart and be gone.
Nightacott, Narracott, Hunnacott's passed,
  Right for the North they race:
He's leading them straight for Blackmoor Gate,
  And he's setting a pounding pace!

We're running him now on a breast-high scent,
  But he leaves us standing still;
When we swing round by Westland Pound
  He's far up Challacombe Hill.
The pack are a string of struggling ants,
  The quarry's a dancing midge,
They're trying their reins on the edge of the Chains
  While he's on Cheriton Ridge.

He's gone by Kittuck and Lucott Moor,
  He's gone by Woodcock's Ley;
By the little white town he's turned him down,
  And he's soiling in open sea.
So hurry along, we'll both be in,
  The crowd are a parish away!
We're a field of two, and we've followed it through
From Bratton to Porlock Bay!

  So hurry along, we'll both be in,
    The crowd are a parish away!
  We're a field of two, and we've followed it through
    From Bratton to Porlock Bay!

Fidele's Grassy Tomb

The Squire sat propped in a pillowed chair,
His eyes were alive and clear of care,
But well he knew that the hour was come
To bid good-bye to his ancient home.

He looked on garden, wood, and hill,
He looked on the lake, sunny and still:
The last of earth that his eyes could see
Was the island church of Orchardleigh.

The last that his heart could understand
Was the touch of the tongue that licked his hand:
"Bury the dog at my feet," he said,
And his voice dropped, and the Squire was dead.

Now the dog was a hound of the Danish breed,
Staunch to love and strong at need:
He had dragged his master safe to shore
When the tide was ebbing at Elsinore.

From that day forth, as reason would,
He was named "Fidele," and made it good:
When the last of the mourners left the door
Fidele was dead on the chantry floor.

They buried him there at his master's feet,
And all that heard of it deemed it meet:
The story went the round for years,
Till it came at last to the Bishop's ears.

Bishop of Bath and Wells was he,
Lord of the lords of Orchardleigh;
And he wrote to the Parson the strongest screed
That Bishop may write or Parson read.

The sum of it was that a soulless hound
Was known to be buried in hallowed ground:
From scandal sore the Church to save
They must take the dog from his masters grave.

The heir was far in a foreign land,
The Parson was wax to my Lord's command:
He sent for the Sexton and bade him make
A lonely grave by the shore of the lake.

The Sexton sat by the water's brink
Where he used to sit when he used to think:
He reasoned slow, but he reasoned it out,
And his argument left him free from doubt.

"A Bishop," he said, "is the top of his trade:
But there's others can give him a start with the spade:
Yon dog, he carried the Squire ashore,
And a Christian couldn't ha' done no more.

The grave was dug; the mason came
And carved on stone Fidele's name;
But the dog that the Sexton laid inside
Was a dog that never had lived or died.

So the Parson was praised,and the scandal stayed,
Till, a long time after, the church decayed,
And, laying the floor anew, they found
In the tomb of the Squire the bones of a hound.

As for the Bishop of Bath and Wells
No more of him the story tells;
Doubtless he lived as a Prelate and Prince,
And died and was buried a century since.

And whether his view was right or wrong
Has little to do with this my song;
Something we owe him, you must allow;
And perhaps he has changed his mind by now.

The Squire in the family chantry sleeps,
The marble still his memory keeps:
Remember, when the name you spell,
There rest Fidele's bones as well.

For the Sexton's grave you need not search,
'Tis a nameless mound by the island church:
An ignorant fellow, of humble lot—-
But. he knew one thing that a Bishop did not.

Moonset

Past seven o'clock: time to be gone;
Twelfth-night's over and dawn shivering up:
A hasty cut of the loaf, a steaming cup,
Down to the door, and there is Coachman John.

Ruddy of cheek is John and bright of eye;
But John it appears has none of your grins and winks;
Civil enough, but short: perhaps he thinks:
Words come once in a mile, and always dry.

Has he a mind or not? I wonder; but soon
We turn through a leafless wood, and there to the right,
Like a sun bewitched in alien realms of night,
Mellow and yellow and rounded hangs the moon.

Strangely near she seems, and terribly great:
The world is dead: why are we travelling still?
Nightmare silence grips my struggling will;
We are driving for ever and ever to find a gate.

"When you come to consider the moon," says John at last,
And stops, to feel his footing and take his stand;
"And then there's some will say there's never a hand
That made the world!"
            A flick, and the gates are passed.

Out of the dim magical moonlit park,
Out to the workday road and wider skies:
There's a warm flush in the East where day's to rise,
And I'm feeling the better for Coachman John's remark.

Master And Man

Do ye ken hoo to fush for the salmon?
  If ye'll listen I'll tell ye.
Dinna trust to the books and their gammon,
  They're but trying to sell ye.
Leave professors to read their ain cackle
  And fush their ain style;
Come awa', sir, we'll oot wi' oor tackle
  And be busy the while.

'Tis a wee bit ower bright, ye were thinkin'?
  Aw, ye'll no be the loser;
'Tis better ten baskin' and blinkin'
  Than ane that's a cruiser.
If ye're bent, as I tak it, on slatter,
  Ye should pray for the droot,
For the salmon's her ain when there's watter,
  But she's oors when it's oot.

Ye may just put your flee-book behind ye,
  Ane hook wull be plenty;
If they'll no come for this, my man, mind ye,
  They'll no come for twenty.
Ay, a rod; but the shorter the stranger
  And the nearer to strike;
For myself I prefare it nae langer
  Than a yard or the like.

Noo, ye'll stand awa' back while I'm creepin'
  Wi' my snoot i' the gowans;
There's a bonny twelve-poonder a-sleepin'
  I' the shade o' yon rowans.
Man, man! I was fearin' I'd stirred her,
  But I've got her the noo!
Hoot! fushin's as easy as murrder
  When ye ken what to do.

Na, na, sir, I doot na ye're willin'
  But I canna permit ye;
For I'm thinkin' that yon kind o' killin'
  Wad hardly befit ye.

And some work is deefficult hushin',
  There'd be havers and chaff:
'Twull be best, sir, for you to be fushin'
  And me wi' the gaff.

Gavotte

(Old French)

Memories long in music sleeping,
  No more sleeping,
    No more dumb;
Delicate phantoms softly creeping
  Softly back from the old-world come.

Faintest odours around them straying,
  Suddenly straying
    In chambers dim;
Whispering silks in order swaying,
  Glimmering gems on shoulders slim:

Courage advancing strong and tender,
  Grace untender
    Fanning desire;
Suppliant conquest, proud surrender,
  Courtesy cold of hearts on fire—-

Willowy billowy now they're bending,
  Low they're bending
    Down-dropt eyes;
Stately measure and stately ending,
  Music sobbing, and a dream that dies.

Imogen

(A Lady of Tender Age)

Ladies, where were your bright eyes glancing,
  Where were they glancing yester-night?
Saw ye Imogen dancing, dancing,
  Imogen dancing all in white?
  Laughed she not with a pure delight,
  Laughed she not with a joy serene,
Stepped she not with a grace entrancing,
  Slenderly girt in silken sheen?

All through the night from dusk to daytime
  Under her feet the hours were swift,
Under her feet the hours of play-time
  Rose and fell with a rhythmic lift:
  Music set her adrift, adrift,
  Music eddying towards the day
Swept her along as brooks in May-time
  Carry the freshly falling May.

Ladies, life is a changing measure,
  Youth is a lilt that endeth soon;
Pluck ye never so fast at pleasure
  Twilight follows the longest noon.
  Nay, but here is a lasting boon,
  Life for hearts that are old and chill,
Youth undying for hearts that treasure
  Imogen dancing, dancing still.

Nel Mezzo Del Cammin

Whisper it not that late in years
Sorrow shall fade and the world be brighter,
Life be freed of tremor and tears,
Heads be wiser and hearts be lighter.
Ah! but the dream that all endears,
The dream we sell for your pottage of truth—-
Give us again the passion of youth,
Sorrow shall fade and the world be brighter.

The Invasion

Spring, they say, with his greenery
  Northward marches at last,
    Mustering thorn and elm;
Breezes rumour him conquering,
  Tell how Victory sits
    High on his glancing helm.

Smit with sting of his archery,
  Hardest ashes and oaks
    Burn at the root below:
Primrose, violet, daffodil,
  Start like blood where the shafts
    Light from his golden bow.

Here where winter oppresses us
  Still we listen and doubt,
    Dreading a hope betrayed:
Sore we long to be greeting him,
  Still we linger and doubt
    "What if his march be stayed?"

Folk in thrall to the enemy,
  Vanquished, tilling a soil
    Hateful and hostile grown;
Always wearily, warily,
  Feeding deep in the heart
    Passion they dare not own—-

So we wait the deliverer;
  Surely soon shall he come,
    Soon shall his hour be due:
Spring shall come with his greenery,
  Life be lovely again,
    Earth be the home we knew.

Pereunt Et Imputantur

(After Martial)

Bernard, if to you and me
  Fortune all at once should give
Years to spend secure and free,
  With the choice of how to live,
Tell me, what should we proclaim
Life deserving of the name?

Winning some one else's case?
  Saving some one else's seat?
Hearing with a solemn face
  People of importance bleat?
No, I think we should not still
Waste our time at others' will.

Summer noons beneath the limes,
  Summer rides at evening cool,
Winter's tales and home-made rhymes,
  Figures on the frozen pool—-
These would we for labours take,
And of these our business make.

Ah! but neither you nor I
  Dare in earnest venture so;
Still we let the good days die
  And to swell the reckoning go.
What are those that know the way,
Yet to walk therein delay?

Felix Antonius

(After Martial)

To-day, my friend is seventy-five;
  He tells his tale with no regret;
  His brave old eyes are steadfast yet,
His heart the .lightest heart alive.

He sees behind him green and wide
  The pathway of his pilgrim years;
  He sees the shore, and dreadless hears
The whisper of the creeping tide.

For out of all his days, not one
  Has passed and left its unlaid ghost
  To seek a light for ever lost,
Or wail a deed for ever done.

So for reward of life-long truth
  He lives again, as good men can,
  Redoubling his allotted span
With memories of a stainless youth.

Ireland, Ireland

Down thy valleys, Ireland, Ireland,
  Down thy valleys green and sad,
Still thy spirit wanders wailing,
  Wanders wailing, wanders mad.

Long ago that anguish took thee,
  Ireland, Ireland, green and fair,
Spoilers strong in darkness took thee,
  Broke thy heart and left thee there.

Down thy valleys, Ireland, Ireland,
  Still thy spirit wanders mad;
All too late they love that wronged thee,
  Ireland, Ireland, green and sad.

Hymn

In The Time Of War And Tumults

O Lord Almighty, Thou whose hands
  Despair and victory give;
In whom, though tyrants tread their lands,
  The souls of nations live;

Thou wilt not turn Thy face away
  From those who work Thy will,
But send Thy peace on hearts that pray,
  And guard Thy people still.

Remember not the days of shame,
  The hands with rapine dyed,
The wavering will, the baser aim,
  The brute material pride:

Remember, Lord, the years of faith,
  The spirits humbly brave,
The strength that died defying death,
  The love that loved the slave:

The race that strove to rule Thine earth
  With equal laws unbought: .
Who bore for Truth the pangs of birth,
  And brake the bonds of Thought.

Remember how, since time began,
  Thy dark eternal mind
Through lives of men that fear not man
  Is light for all mankind.

Thou wilt not turn Thy face away
  From those who work Thy will,
But send Thy strength on hearts that pray
  For strength to serve Thee still.

The Building Of The Temple

(An Anthem Heard In Canterbury Cathedral)

[The Organ]

O Lord our God, we are strangers before Thee, and sojourners, as were all our fathers: our days on the earth are as a shadow, and there is none abiding.

O Lord God of our fathers, keep this for ever in the imagination of the thoughts of Thy people, and prepare their heart unto Thee.

And give unto Solomon my son a perfect heart to keep Thy commandments, and to build the palace for the which I have made provision.

[Boys' voices.]

O come to the Palace of Life,
Let us build it again.
It was founded on terror and strife,
It was laid in the curse of the womb,
And pillared on toil and pain,
And hung with veils of doom,
And vaulted with the darkness of the tomb.

[Men's voices.]

O Lord our God, we are sojourners here for a day,
  Strangers and sojourners, as all our fathers were:
Our years on the earth are a shadow that fadeth away;
  Grant us light for our labour, and a time for prayer.

[Boys.]

But now with endless song,
And joy fulfilling the Law;
Of passion as pure as strong
And pleasure undimmed of awe;
With garners of wine and grain
Laid up for the ages long,

Let us build the Palace again
And enter with endless song,
Enter and dwell secure, forgetting the years of wrong.

[Men.]

O Lord our God, we are strangers and sojourners here,
  Our beginning was night, and our end is hid in Thee:
Our labour on the earth is hope redeeming fear,
  In sorrow we build for the days we shall not see.

[Boys.]

Great is the name
Of the strong and skilled,
Lasting the fame
Of them that build:
The tongues of many nations
Shall speak of our praise,
And far generations
Be glad for our days.

[Men.]

We are sojourners here as all our fathers were,
  As all our children shall be, forgetting and forgot:
The fame of man is a murmur that passeth on the air,
  We perish indeed if Thou remember not.

We are sojourners here as all our fathers were,
  Strangers travelling down to the land of death:
There is neither work nor device nor knowledge there,
  O grant us might for our labour, and to rest in faith.

[Boys.]

In joy, in the joy of the light to be,

[Men.]

  O Father of Lights, unvarying and true,

[Boys.]

Let us build the Palace of Life anew.

[Men.]

  Let us build for the years we shall not see.

[Boys.]

Lofty of line and glorious of hue,
With gold and pearl and with the cedar tree,

[Men.]

  With silence due
  And with service free,

[Boys.]

Let us build it for ever in splendour new.

[Men.]

  Let us build in hope and in sorrow, and rest in Thee.

NOTES

Drake's Drum.

A state drum, painted with the arms of Sir Francis Drake, is preserved among other relics at Buckland Abbey, the seat ofthe Drake family in Devon.

The Fighting Téméraire.

The two last stanzas have been misunderstood.
It seems, therefore, necessary to state that they are intended to refer to Turner's picture in the National Gallery of "The Fighting *Téméraire* Tugged to her Last Berth."

San Stefano.

Sir Peter Parker was the son of Admiral Christopher Parker, grandson of Admiral Sir Peter Parker (the life-long friend and chief mourner of Nelson), and great-grandson of Admiral Sir William Parker. On his mother's side he was grandson of Admiral Byron, and first cousin of Lord Byron, the poet. He was killed in action near Baltimore in 1814, and buried in St. Margaret's, Westminster, where may be seen the monument erected to his memory by the officers of the *Menelaus*.

The Quarter-Gunner's Yarn.

This ballad is founded on fragmentary lines communicated to the author by Admiral Sir Windham Hornby, K.C.B., who served under Sir Thomas Hardy in 1827.

Væ Victis.

See *Livy*, XXX.,43, *Diodorus Siculus*, XIX., 106.

Seringapatam.

In 1780, while attempting to relieve Arcot, a British force of three thousand men was cut to pieces by Hyder Ali. Baird, then a young captain in the 73rd, was left for dead on the field. He was afterwards, with forty-nine other officers, kept in prison at Seringapatam, and treated with Oriental barbarity and treachery by Hyder Ali and his son Tippoo Sahib, Sultans of Mysore. Twenty-three of the prisoners died by poison, torture, and fever; the rest were surrendered in 1784. In 1799, at the siege of Seringapatam, Major-General Baird commanded the first European brigade, and volunteered to lead the storming column. Tippoo Sahib, with eight thousand of his men, fell in the assault, but the victor spared the lives of his sons and forbade a general sack of the city.

Clifton Chapel.

Clifton is one of the schools from which the largest number of boys pass direct into the R.M.A., Woolwich, and R.M.C., Sandhurst. Thirty-five Old Cliftonian officers served in the campaign of 1897 on the Indian Frontier, of whom twenty-two were mentioned in despatches and six recommended for the Distinguished Service Order. Of the three hundred Cliftonians who served in the war in South Africa, thirty were killed in action and fourteen died of wounds or fever.

Clifton, remember these thy sons who fell
  Fighting far oversea;
 For they in a dark hour remembered well
  Their warfare learned of thee.

The Echo.

The ballad was "The Twa Sisters of Binnorie," as set by Arthur Somervell.

THE END.

Lightning Source UK Ltd.
Milton Keynes UK
15 October 2010

161332UK00001B/126/A